DISCARD

SIMPLE SIGNS

Cindy Wheeler

VIKING

To my son, Will

VIKING
Published by the Penguin Group
Penguin Books USA Inc., 375 Hudson Street, New York, New York 10014, U.S.A.
Penguin Books Ltd, 27 Wrights Lane, London W8 5TZ, England
Penguin Books Australia Ltd, Ringwood, Victoria, Australia
Penguin Books Canada Ltd, 10 Alcorn Avenue, Toronto, Ontario, Canada M4V 3B2
Penguin Books (N.Z.) Ltd, 182–190 Wairau Road, Auckland 10, New Zealand

Penguin Books Ltd, Registered Offices: Harmondsworth, Middlesex, England

First published in 1995 by Viking, a division of Penguin Books USA Inc.

5 7 9 10 8 6 4

Copyright © Cindy Wheeler, 1995
All rights reserved

Library of Congress Cataloging-in-Publication Data
Wheeler, Cindy.
Simple signs / Cindy Wheeler.
p.   cm.
Includes bibliographical references.
Summary: Demonstrates through illustrations and brief text twenty-nine
American Sign Language signs for words such as hello, cry, dog, and love.
ISBN 0-670-86282-7
1. American Sign Language—Juvenile literature.   [1. Sign language.]   I. Title.
HV2476.W48   1995   419—dc20   95-11141   CIP   AC

Printed in China
Set in Tekton

Author's Note

My son, Will, was born with Down Syndrome. As is typical of such kids, Will's speech came very slowly, and when he was about one year old his speech therapist began teaching him American Sign Language (ASL). By the time Will was eighteen months old, he knew how to sign that he wanted to "eat" or "sleep." He was able to sign that he wanted "more" or that he was "finished." And he could sign that he loved me.

As my daughter, my husband, and I learned ASL with Will, we became impressed with the beauty—and the simplicity—of the signs. Some children learn to sign the alphabet when they reach school age. But word-signs are accessible even to preschoolers who do not yet know the alphabet. The appeal is much the same as that of finger plays such as "Eentsy-Weentsy Spider." The benefits are without number.

Simple Signs is my tribute to the language that let me communicate with my son.

If you would like to know more about ASL, here are some of the resources I used in preparing this book:

Benjamin Bahan, Joe Dannis, and Frank Paul. *Signs for Me: A Basic Sign Language for Children, Parents & Teachers.* Dawn Sign Press, 1987.

Elaine Costello. *Random House American Sign Language Dictionary.* Random House, Inc., 1994.

Lottie Riekehof. *The Joy of Signing.* Gospel Publishing House, 1987.

hello

hint: like saluting

hint: show a cat's
whiskers

cat

dog

hint: pat
your leg as if
calling a dog

hint: like holding a ball

ball

car

hint: like driving a car

hint: like milking a cow

milk

banana

hint: like peeling a banana

hint: like using a
cookie cutter

cookie

eat

hint: like putting food
in your mouth

hint: touch fingertips
together

more

finished

hint: like brushing crumbs
off your shirt

hint: make a loop up
from your heart

happy

cry

hint: show falling tears
with fingertips

1.

2.

hint: like opening
a book

music

hint: like
conducting music

baby

hint: like rocking a baby

mother & father

mother
hint:
thumb
on
chin

father
hint:
thumb
on forehead

bird

hint: fingers open and
close like a bird's beak

COW

hint: stick out little finger
like a cow's horn and
wag it up and down

hint: like a butterfly's wings fluttering

butterfly

turtle

hint: curve top hand like
a shell, wiggle thumb
like a turtle's head

snake

hint: shape fingers
like fangs, move
hands like a snake

elephant

hint: show
an elephant's trunk

1.

2.

hint: index fingers hook
one way then the other

friend

bicycle

hint: like pedaling
a bicycle

hint: make hand
into a C-shape like
a crescent moon

moon

sleep

hint: like eyes
being closed

hint: like a hug

love